FREEDOM, TRIBALISM, AND CREATIVITY: A CHALLENGE TO OUR SYRIAN FRIENDS

JOHN FREEMAN, M.D.
C. BEN MITCHELL, PH.D.

FREEDOM, TRIBALISM, AND CREATIVITY:
A Challenge to Our Syrian Friends
By: John Freeman, M.D. & C. Ben Mitchell, Ph.D.

All rights reserved. Except for brief exerpts for review purposes, no part of this book may be reproduced or used in any form without written permission from the author.

ISBN-13: 978-1495454059
ISBN-10: 1495454053

© 2012 John D. Freeman & C. Ben Mitchell
All Rights Reserved.

Cover and Layout Design: Ryan Oetting
Cover Image: John Freeman.
Image of "Baghdad Bob's Tourist Stop" between Damascas and Palmyra.

Printed in the United States of America

My first contact with the Middle East was at the University of Texas where I had Arab roommates. Through their gracious hospitality, I was made an unofficial member of the Arab Students Association. Later in my career, I spent time in Saudi Arabia doing rural medical work. The events of late have fostered an intense interest in that part of the world. In discussing the problems of the Middle East with my good friend Ben Mitchell, a professor of moral philosophy, we came up with the concept of the "moral imperative in the creative nature of God" as a solution to the problems of the Middle East. Ben and I spent many mornings at breakfast discussing the issue and this little document is the result.

Several friends have been gracious enough to critique and correct the manuscript and a hearty thanks to them. Those friends include; Glenn Deckert, Donald Gold, Kevin Chiarot, Walton Padelford, and Joyce VanDuesen.

FORWARD

I first met John Freeman at a public lecture on my university's campus. We promised to meet again—and we did—many times after that. I'm very grateful to be able to call John a friend. Our friendship was formed around ideas. John is a clear thinker and a man of vast life-experience, having practiced as a physician in a number of exotic places in the developing world.

As you will learn in this book, John Freeman was "adopted" into an Arabic community while he was in college. From that time onward, his love and appreciation deepened for the people of the world, especially the people in the Middle

East. This book is, in a sense, a love letter to his global family.

The word "tribalism" in the title will strike some readers as odd, perhaps even off-putting. It is not meant to be so. Rather, it is a sociological description of a way of life that is separatist, parochial, and sectarian. The argument of the book is that tribalism is stultifying to freedom, creativity, and genuine progress. Throughout the Middle East—in Syria, Iraq, Egypt, and Lebanon—people are crying out for "freedom!" The point John makes is that freedom and tribalism are not compatible.

With all of its faults, the West has been shaped in the crucible of freedom. The formative power of personal liberty has resulted in one of the most, if not the most, creative and productive cultures in the history of civilization. Many children have been birthed from freedom's womb: liberal democracy, limited powers of government, protection of human dignity, religious freedom, racial and gender equality, reward for productive labor, modern science, and much, much more.

Both Dr. Freeman and I long to see the benefits of freedom enjoyed by a world currently enslaved under despotic rule. We are not Pollyannas, however. We realize that freedom often comes at great cost. Yet for the refreshing winds of the

Arab Spring to achieve their ends, tribalism must come to an end. In order for individuals and cultures to fan the flames of creativity, sectarianism will have to give way to democracy. Our hope is that this little book will find its way into the hands of our Middle Eastern friends wherever freedom's cry is heard. We stand with them in the quest for liberty, creativity, and human flourishing.

C. Ben Mitchell, Ph.D.
Graves Professor of Moral Philosophy
Union University

INTRODUCTION
-CHAPTER 1-

A friend and I were discussing the pressing problems of the Middle East and the need for creative thinking about solutions when the phrase, "the moral imperative in the creative nature of God," came up. We decided to develop that thought with the aim in mind of offering help to our Arab and Muslim friends. Based on the background of my work and travel in various places — where tribalism is the natural order of the culture — we try to describe the problem requiring the solution inherent in the concept of "the moral imperative in the creative nature of God."

In my lifetime there have been several brutal autocratic

tribal systems that have sought to impose their ideology on the subject peoples with devastating results. In Korea in the mid fifties as a young soldier I observed the impoverished Koreans as they scratched together anything and everything to start rebuilding their society and country. Another Communist crime that I came in contact with was the "Killing Fields of Cambodia," when, as the medical coordinator of a refugee camp in 1981, I saw the suffering of a people brutalized by the attempt to impose a Communist "tribal" system. In our training program in Peshawar in 1987, we drew our patients from an Afghan refugee camp of fifty thousand homeless Afghans with no certain future, all because the Russian Communists were out to impose their brand of tribalism on another people.

For several years I worked to bring healthcare to tribal people along the Thai-Burma border. It was there that I heard and saw the results of the brutal hand of the Burmese government, which resulted in the displacement of tens of thousands of innocent villagers and the destruction of thousands of villages. This was all done to keep in power a vicious autocratic regime that sought to impose a rigid tribal-like culture.

CHAPTER 1

The mass slaughter of the Tutsis and the Hutus in Rwanda still haunts my memory, as hundreds of thousands were mercilessly killed in a rampage of one tribe trying to extinguish the other.

My travels have taken me to India where certain groups of people are called "untouchables" and relegated to permanent poverty. That seems to be the result of a religiously institutionalized "tribal" system. The Islamic concept of dhimmitude is another aspect of enforced second-class citizenship, which is inherent in its own "tribal" system. In Saudi Arabia the enforcement of the tribal system did not allow for a Saudi to become a Christian or any other religion. While working in Abha-Khamis, the public beheadings in the square following Friday prayers reminded us of the rigidly enforced tribalism. America has had its time of dehumanizing second-class citizenship in the form of slavery, which was finally, in a cataclysmic event, eliminated. Following that event were years of segregation, and today that problem is largely resolved.

Man's journey from a primitive tribal system to a system of free autonomous self-regulating individuals has been a slow and painful process. Such tribal systems in early hostile environments were necessary for survival. The Greeks managed to break free of tribalism as they developed a search for truth. Phenomenal accomplishments resulted from their break from tribalism. Christians picked up the mantle and marched forward with the words of Christ, "ye shall know the truth and the truth shall make you free", inspiring them to appropriate the creative nature of God.

The sad fact is that the seeds of tribalism, with the desire to lord it over others, seem to connect with a dominant factor in human nature. When truth is scarce, there is always another force to take its place, and that is the imposition of a tribal system. Examples of such are communism, fascism, and Nazism all brands of a socialist style of tribalism with their own names. Those were political systems, but religious systems have their own imposed systems of tribalism as well.

This essay is an attempt to develop a progression from tribalism to a system where the moral imperative in the creative nature of God may work to correct the ills of society in the Middle East.

THE CRY FOR FREEDOM
-CHAPTER 2-

A friend and I were trekking through the Asir hills of Saudi Arabia when we came upon a party in the desert. We had no idea what they were celebrating, so we decided to skirt around the group, partly out of respect and partly in self-defense. But shouts from the camp indicated that we were being invited to join them. As we drew near, I noticed that the wife had no head covering and that the children were playing about the thorn bush from which was hanging a freshly skinned goat ready for roasting. The father motioned for us to sit beside him near the open fire where tea was already prepared and waiting. Although the wife did most of the talking, we did not understand Arabic and they did not understand English. But we drew pictures on the ground and made hand gestures while sipping the hot cardamom tea. To Arabs, hospitality is hospitality, whether or not you enjoy a common language. That unexpected experience has remained with me ever since, like a precious jewel that gives me great pleasure each time I look back at it.

That mother of the young Saudi family was, in all probability, engaging for the first time in conversation with men from another world. We could sense great pleasure in inquiring about our wives and children and sharing with us about her children who were by now hovering around the fire listening raptly to the "conversation." In the isolation of the desert, and without the sequestering burka, this little family had for a brief period enjoyed what most people around the world would consider a normal situation.

In an earlier time as a young soldier in Korea I had the occasion to meet with some young Korean men who were also interested in joining the modern world. They had grown up under a severe Japanese imperialism, as their land had been totally devastated by a prolonged war between the communist north and the UN forces. Learning English was

CHAPTER 2

one of their avenues to experience a modern world and I was their teacher. These young men, and thousands like them, were successful in creating a modern state and free culture. Today South Korea is one of the great industrial nations leading the world in shipbuilding. When they started making automobiles a few years ago, their vehicles were a laughing matter, but now they compete with the finest made anywhere.

In 1993, while conducting a medical survey, I encountered a crude camp on the Burmese side of the Salween River. The leader of the group was pointed out to me as the young man lying on a crude bench in the sun. He was sleeping, while at the same time having a malaria chill. He finally roused himself to engage us in conversation. His group had been leaders in the democracy protest in Rangoon in 1991. Their noble and gallant attempt to join the modern world was quashed by the ruthless Burmese military government and for the intervening time, these who had once aspired to a good education and meaningful jobs were reduced to foraging in the jungle for their food and suffering the ravages of jungle diseases. To this day Burma is a backward, decrepit country.

The young medical workers in Peshawar we were training in 1987 to return to Afghanistan to establish clinics, offered me another picture of a yearning to join the modern world. Those young Afghan men and women were among the brightest and most energetic young people I have known. Yet I wonder where they have ended up, as their country is still wracked by discord and war.

The interpreters we had in our medical clinics in the Asir region of Saudi Arabia came from Yemen, Lebanon, Egypt, and other places of the Middle East. They had come from countries with few opportunities, so many of them appealed to us doctors to help them get to our countries. They, too, wanted to partake of the modern world where tribalism is not a dominant factor. Their countries are still backward and presently in the midst of chaos and turmoil.

My latest encounter with young people wanting to be part of the modern world was in south Syria in 2005. My driver on that visit insisted that I visit his village in the Al Suweida area. His college-age brothers, sisters, and cousins hovered around me drinking in every word that fell from my lips. I was treated like a long-lost rich uncle, and probably was the first westerner to visit their village in their lifetimes. The brightness of their countenances was such a contrast to the drab oppressive atmosphere of Damascus and Homs where

I had visited. As I left they begged me to return and bring my wife. I felt that I had made lifelong friends in that village. With the turmoil and killing in Syria in 2011, I wonder what has happened to my friends who were longing for freedom and a chance to live a "normal" life.

PRESENT OPPRESSION

Bernard Lewis, one of the most renowned scholars of the Arab world, has recently written *The End of Modern History in the Middle East*. My own introduction to the modern history of the Middle East was at the University of Texas in the fifties when there were a large number of students from that part of the world. At times I had roommates from Homs, Syria, and Saudi Arabia. Consequently, I became an unofficial member of the Arab Students Association and was invited to all their functions. That was a time when in the Middle East, and among my colleagues, there was openness to the modern world and expectations that their countries would actually become part of that world. Lebanon was a stable and prosperous little country that in those days was held up as the jewel of the Mediterranean. Egypt aspired to become a nation equal in modernity to the European group of nations.

My roommate from Homs obtained his engineering degree and returned to a successful career in Syria, but the spring of hope and aspiration toward a free and open society in his and the other Arab countries quickly faded as political power fell into the hands of autocrats. The saga of how that spring turned winter is told in *The Dream Palace of the Arabs* by Fouad Ajami, who tells of the sad fate of those Arab reformers who struggled to bring free thought and expression to the Arab World. Among those rays that shone the light of hope to that early Arab Spring were the likes of Saadah, Hawi, Qabbani, Adonis, Baghdadi, Foda, Mahfuz, and others. They were crushed like flowers under the brutal hand of fundamentalists, but the fragrance of their visions lingers to inspire those of the present spring, thanks to the writings of Ajami and others.

For the past fifty years I have known of a Middle East which has been defined by stagnation and oppression. Education has been provided to the burgeoning population of youth but, contrary to what my Homs roommate found, a career for them is now but a faded dream. During my trip to Damascus five years ago, I found a city that seemed to be stained by tears of disappointment and despair. While in Jordan

CHAPTER 2

visiting Petra with my son, a group of South Asians caught his eye. They were textile workers imported to staff Jordanian factories. The recent conflict in Libya sent thousands of foreign workers scurrying from that place. Why import labor when unemployment is such a problem? Clearly something seems amiss when, in the face of high unemployment, foreign labor replaces locals.

The Syrian economy is the size of Pittsburgh's, yet it has over twenty million people. Several of my Arab friends have targeted colonial oppression as the cause of the backwardness of the Middle East economies, but look at the success of the Korean economy, which has risen from the ashes of a scorched earth Japanese imperialism and a devastating civil war, plus losing a generation of their young. Another indicator of problems in the Middle East is that "the total exports other than fossil fuels of the Arab world plus Iran amount to less than those of Finland." (Lewis, *The End of Modern History*, p. 48). The tiny state of Israel has won more Nobel prizes than the entire Arab world. More books are translated yearly from English into Spanish than translated into Arabic by all the Arab states. These are only a few of the indicators of the serious problems that exist in the Arab world.

Thirty years ago Fouad Ajami wrote about the time period that we are here discussing in the book *The Arab Predicament* in which he analyzes Arab political thought and practice. A native of Lebanon and fluent in Arabic, Ajami quotes extensively the Arabic men of letters who introspectively examine the difficulties Arabs confront as they seek to enter the modern world of free thought and actions. Bernard Lewis has just authored another book documenting the multiple problems facing the Arab Middle East of today (*The End of Modern History in the Middle East*). Mr. Lewis writes with the weight of almost 90 years immersion in the Arab culture of which he is a foremost authority. To our Arab friends who aspire to enter the modern free world, we encourage the reading of the works of Ajami and Lewis.

The first cries heard from the Syrian protesters in 2011 were "Freedom! Freedom! Freedom!" We voice our hope that this is truly the beginning of an Arab Spring which will bring us from the dark winter of the past fifty plus years. Optimism is born by the flight of several of the autocrats who have wielded such a heavy hand of oppression. Whatever reason they gave for their repressions, the people have finally had enough and their actions brought results. The struggle is still not over and,

CHAPTER 2

in fact, may have just started. The early and late spring frosts may yet wither the new buds of freedom and hope. Already in Egypt there have been killings of Christians and burning of churches with threats of more. The vicious weeds of a violent fundamentalism are already thriving in places where the Arab Spring has allowed growing conditions.

Just as a garden needs frequent weeding, there is hope of seeing this as some of the protesters' posters from Syria read, "Terrorism No. Yes to Freedom". Another poster read "No to Iran and No to Hezbollah. Yes to Freedom." Thus from the Syrian protesters there is indication that the choking weeds of Fundamentalism are recognized and hopefully can be uprooted and left for the burning pile, just as the weeds of heavy handed autocracy are being uprooted.

As some autocrats have been chased from the Middle East, others are now talking of democratic reform. There are hopes that Fundamentalist terror is being recognized as the evil it is and becoming unwelcome. Tribalism is another issue that confronts the Middle Easterners and will be a serious obstacle in the development of a unified democratic society. The brilliant success of South Korea is based to a large extent on the fact that it is a unified society with no tribes to distract.

The misery in both Burma and Afghanistan is rooted, to a great deal, in the society being divided by tribalism.

WHAT IS FREEDOM?
-CHAPTER 3-

The Syrian protest movement started with the cry, "Freedom! Freedom! Freedom!" We need to stop to ask, "Just what is freedom?" One dissident was quoted as saying, "I want freedom to do what you consider normal." Trying to define freedom reminds one of Buddha as he tried to define Nirvana, the Buddhist heaven. He could only tell his followers what Nirvana was not. To many Syrians of the protest movement freedom is defined as a country without Bashar Assad. It is a country without a corrupt government. There are many other negatives that could be added in order to try to define freedom. But there are also great positives that mark a free state.

Personal autonomy, for instance, should be the natural or normal state of the individual in a free society. The spontaneous and phenomenally widespread push for the "natural state" in Syria is truly amazing to behold. There, the cry is heard of tens of thousands speaking in a unified pulsating yearning to break free from the shackles of an oppressive autocratic system. The most obvious factor involved in striping autonomy from the Syrians is the corrupt political system. The fundamental fact is that any ruling order that imposes a multitude of rules and regulations acts as a constraint on individual freedom.

The sixth-century Chinese philosopher, Laozi, has been quoted as saying, "The more prohibitions there are, the poorer the people become." The more rules the more individuals must be enlisted to enforce the rules, thus creating a set of citizens who are above those to whom the rules apply. There is an inevitable tendency for the enforcers of rules to develop their own subsets of rules. In the end the rules and regulations become so complicated that suppression of innovation and free thought results in stagnation of society. Saad, my Saudi roommate, extolled his religious system as having a rule for every detail of life, making for a very structured society and

CHAPTER 3

comforting in its own way; but as anyone knows who has lived and worked in the kingdom of Saudi Arabia, it is a very constricted society in terms of individual freedom. About five or six years ago I watched a CNN special on Saudi Arabia in which a young man was interviewed. Having learned English quite well by watching TV, the interview was in English. He listed the restrictions his society had placed on him and ended the interview by asking the question, "Why do I have to live like this?"

We have lately been reading the stated objectives of Hezbollah, The Muslim Brotherhood, and Hamas, all of whom are vying for leadership in the present "Arab Spring." If their goals are achieved by gaining the dominance in the protest movement, then we may find ourselves rescued from the mouth of the autocratic dictators only to slip into the jaws of a worse system, which is a backward system including the slavery of an institutionalized religious tribal system with its constricting rules for every facet of life.

Escape from institutionalized tribalism into the free world is not an easy task. A mullah in the Russian state of Dagestan found this to be true the other day as he was shot in the head for advocating a relaxed attitude toward the use of the burka. Honor killings, so common in the Middle East, are yet another glaring example of the grip that an institutionalized tribal system can hold on its subjects.

Early in our recorded history we have the story of how God took Abraham by the hand and told him to "Leave your country, your people, and your father's household to a place I will show you." Abraham is considered one of the most important prophets of the Jews, Christians, and Muslims; therefore we may use his example as we follow his trek from tribalism to freedom. Note first that it was God who led him to leave his tribal system. By leaving he was not doing anything that would bring dishonor to his father and people for he was doing what many others have done when a land becomes overpopulated.

God led Abraham away from his tribal system in order that Abraham might stand in the presence of God in a direct personal relationship and so comprehend the true nature of the Divine Presence. When Abraham had his feet planted in the new land to which he had been called, God appeared to him and pronounced a blessing on him, telling him that in turn "all peoples would be blessed through you." It is in discovering the full depth of meaning in this injunction to

CHAPTER 3

Abraham that we may find the route to true freedom from the bondage and shackles of the various forms of tribalism that oppress in so many parts of the world.

The God of Abraham thus revealed himself as a God of the moral imperative. That is exactly what is implied in the commission given to Abraham to "be a blessing to all peoples." Such thinking is diametrically opposed to the insular and self-preservation mode of a tribal system. The tribal system fragments and isolates societies, whereas the imperative to "bless others" is a unifying force. Not only does it unify but, it frees us from the bondage of revenge so prevalent in a tribal system.

The narrative in the Old Testament demonstrates that Abraham's "Great Commission" was not easily nor readily instituted by his descendents. God therefore gave other demonstrations to enlighten people about His plan. Moses is a good example of a person stripped of his tribal constraints as he was taken into the household of Pharaoh and then having to flee into the desert to live with the Midianites. It was in the desert that God revealed himself as the God of concern for Moses's people who had become slaves in Egypt. Moses was then incorporated in God's demonstration of concern and compassion as he led the people of Israel out of the slavery of Egypt.

Safely across the Red Sea, Moses recapitulated the commission of Abraham by telling the children of Israel that they were to be priests of God and a holy nation. We may surely imply that the duty of a holy nation was to be a blessing to other nations and that the priests of God imply a nation of individuals standing in a personal relationship to God in order to carry out the duties of "blessing others."

Needless to say, the moral imperative given to Abraham and reiterated to Moses has been difficult to carry out, as the biblical narrative notes. Of course there are many demonstrations of that failure in today's world. A few years ago while on a visit to Israel I engaged an antiquities dealer in discussing the Arab-Israeli problem. The question was posed to him about what the Israelis were doing to reach out to the Arabs. His answer was quite simple: "Nothing!"

The Jewish antiquities dealer had the freedom to do nothing, but true freedom does not exist in a vacuum. The disciples of Buddha inquired as to the nature of Nirvana to which he responded with a series of "it is not this and it is not that." That is of course consistent with one of the core

CHAPTER 3

teaching of Buddhism that of extinguishing all desire. True freedom is not a vessel void of all restraints, but a vessel filled with moral imperatives. To have a country devoid of Assad or Mubarak or Khadafy and to call that freedom is only to erect a false façade.

The basis of a truly free society is in individuals who discover that freedom is not merely the "absence of" but the "presence of." Of course wrong attitudes and habits must be purged, but that is insufficient; our lives must be filled with the "attitude of blessing" revealed to Abraham and the positive attitude of "standing in the presence of God" as Moses decreed to his followers at Mount Sinai.

Eliminating the brutal hand of the autocrats of the Middle East, as filled as it is with struggle and the sacrifice of many lives, will be the easy ingredient in the new mix of freedom. The next great challenge will require even more effort. Leaving behind the smothering tribal system, which has been the inheritance of the Middle East for centuries, will be enormously difficult. The tribal system was there when Abraham was called by God to leave his tribe and go to another land. The constraining tribal ethos would not allow the personal interaction necessary for Abraham to hear God's call to venture into a radically new direction, that of being a blessing to all peoples.

Simply comprehending the need for a "radical new direction," much less following the impetus to seek the implementation of a "radical new direction," will be the great challenge of the youth of the new Middle East. Youth here should be emphasized for it will take the vigor and vision of youth to lead in that direction. Leaving behind ancient traditionalism and institutionalized tribalism with all its irrational baggage will be a formidable task.

The examples chosen here to demonstrate the leaving of a tribal system indicate that it is no trivial task. Abraham's voluntary leaving his tribe at God's command led to a journey that was fraught with many difficulties. Joseph was sold into slavery by his brothers and spent years in prison before beginning his rise to prominence in the house of Pharaoh. Moses narrowly escaped death as an infant then, when barely an adult, had to flee into another land where he was a refugee for forty years before leading the people of God out of the slavery of Egypt. Daniel was taken as a prisoner of war becoming a slave servant in the household of the king of Mesopotamia. In all of these cases the stripping of the tribal

CHAPTER 3

constraints allowed them to stand in the presence of a holy and righteous God and enter into a personal relationship with that God. The personal relationship with God became the source of their moral guidance system that replaced the tribal ethical system from which they came.

Though Abraham was led by God to leave tribalism, Joseph, Moses, and Daniel were forced by circumstances beyond their control to leave the constraints of their tribal systems. In the Middle East today there are many factors creating circumstances that are conducive to leaving the tribal system. Food shortages, unemployment, political upheaval and the emerging forces of radicalism are only some of the factors that require rational inquiry into the solution of the problems facing the Middle Eastern countries. Departure from the tribal system is imperative so that the seeds of innovation and creativity may burst forth to bring a new era.

A new era of freedom will bring about its own challenges for there is the temptation to throw off cultural moral restraints in favor of ones own secular self-interest. A sad example of this is found in Western countries with the rampant sexual promiscuity. The consequent disruption of the family is breeding a multitude of social problems that will be very hard to control. The path of freedom from restraint is a trail littered with personal destruction where discipline is not imposed.

To realize the full essence of freedom there must be acceptance of a moral guidance system found in the examples of Abraham, Joseph, Moses, and Daniel. They all lived in a deep personal relationship with God, which internalized their ethics of righteousness. Of course the Law of Moses found in the Ten Commandments is essential as a standard for society but more important is an internalized moral commitment.

The vacuousness of seizing freedom as liberation from moral restraint in order to pursue self-indulgence could be elaborated on more but there is a greater issue related to freedom that must be explored. Just as tribalism exercises its own constraints, so true freedom, when seen in its fullness, exerts positive moral constraints as developed in the moral imperative given to Abraham in directing him to be a blessing to all peoples. Moses left his people the command to "love your neighbor as yourself." In the story of the Good Samaritan Jesus further defined the neighbor as a person from another tribe. The apostle Paul made reference to the love of God as a constraining force pushing him towards positive action to

CHAPTER 3

others. True freedom at first liberates us and then places us in a harness where we may cultivate the fields of innovation and creativity in solving the problems we as a society face. In such a system all, not only a select few, will be blessed.

FREEDOM CONSTRAINED BY TRIBALISM
-CHAPTER 4-

Is tribalism the future? That is the question Pat Buchannan recently asked in his article discussing the problem of tribalism inherent in the Middle East. And in his book, *The Arab Mind*, Raphael Patai discusses the iron grip that tribalism has and the backwardness it causes in the Middle East. Finally, in his insightful book, *The Arab Predicament*, Fouad Ajami gives many examples of how tribalism with its grip of traditionalism impedes the development of modern thought in their part of the world.

The dominant social system in the Muslim Middle Eastern world is tribalism. This problem is highlighted in

Yemen, Libya, Syria, and Iraq. Interestingly, Iran, not an Arab country though Muslim, seems to be free for the most part from tribalism as it has the unique quality of existing for hundreds of years being unified as a nation state. Most of the present Arab states have boundaries drawn up by the former colonial masters without regard to tribal loyalties. Despite the nature of their origin, the Middle Eastern countries of today consider themselves as legitimate states. The autocrats such as Kaddafi of Libya, Assad of Syria, and Saleh of Yemen justified their heavy handed rule as necessary to keep the disparate tribes unified. A logical concern is that without the strong-handed autocrats those countries will devolve into separate tribal entities. Such a scenario was seen in the case of Yugoslavia when Tito the strongman was deposed.

The tribalism in the Middle East raises the question whether Islam is itself a tribal system. In an informative essay in The Middle East Quarterly, professor of anthropology Philip Carl Salzman, argues that tribalism is part of the Middle East's DNA. Tribal cultures cultivate an "us versus them" mentality in which social segregation, tribal honor, and predatory expansion become the norm. Tribal cultures see themselves set in opposition to others around them. "These groups,"

CHAPTER 4

observes Salzman, "are vested with the responsibility for the defense of each member and are responsible for harm any member does to outsiders." They seek to protect their honor by any means necessary. "Only the victorious have honor. The more vanquished the defeated, the greater is the victor's honor." Tribalist cultures are separationists by definition, often militantly so.

If indeed Islam is a form of institutionalized tribalism then this would complicate the picture. The evidence seems to point to this for when working in Saudi Arabia we found it to be a country with no freedoms of speech, press, assembly, or of religion. My Saudi roommate at the University of Texas informed me that if he returned to his country as a Christian his head would be cut off. While I worked in Saudi Arabia the religious police would walk the streets with a stick, harshly enforcing certain rules about attending the mosque at prayer time or making sure a woman's ankle was adequately covered. Islam seems to have all the hallmarks of a tribal system.

The primitive social structure of tribalism was necessary primarily to protect the tribe in a hostile environment. Food gathering required a group effort as in the case of some American Indians who lived primarily by killing the large bison and the Eskimos whose main foodstuff was the large sea animals. Concern for the survival of the tribe naturally led to an inward and self-centered attitude with a disinterest or even hostility to other tribes who may have been seen as a threat to their well being. When a tribe becomes overpopulated it tends to fragment with the splintered tribe competing for rare food.

Attempts to overcome tribal enmity is seen in the case of modern Burma and Afghanistan both of which are unsuccessful in producing a stable and free society. Saudi Arabia has managed to produce a fairly stable society but not a free one in any modern sense.

Tribalism tends toward a very cohesive social structure with strict discipline and rigid moral codes. To be sure, the insular tribal ethic has good aspects as I observed in the Karen and Wa tribes of Thailand and Burma. After examining a twenty year-old Burmese young lady with symptoms of advanced tuberculosis, I asked my Wa interpreter if it was possible that the girl had by any chance slept with a soldier and perhaps contracted AIDS. "Impossible!" was the emphatic reply, making me feel quite embarrassed that I had even broached the possibility. I changed the subject to inquire about why the rice storage houses were so far from the main house. "In case

CHAPTER 4

of fire," he replied, "the food will not be destroyed." Having noted no locks on the rice bins I suggested theft might be a problem. "There is no stealing in the Wa state," he abruptly stated. The enforcement of a moral society is of course a very good aspect of tribalism. Such an ethic is observed in Japan where a personal object forgotten on public transportation will most certainly be turned in to the authorities to be reclaimed by the owner. In a sense Japan may be considered a tribal society, though all are members of the one national tribe.

In tribalism there is a strong societal need to belong to the tribe. This sense of belonging is so much a part of the society that it often impedes progress. While traveling in rural Costa Rica many years ago I inquired about the absence of home gardens. It was explained that if they planted a garden then the neighbors would come over and help themselves. Again in Thailand, the fruit trees in a yard will be the target of neighbor children when the fruit is ripe. So the sense of belonging and mandatory sharing impedes the planting of gardens and orchards in those regions.

One of the strong detriments of tribal societies is that personal ethics are not developed since tribal morality determines the ethics of the society. Since all the rules and regulations of society are determined by tribal traditions personal autonomy is lost. Tribes tend to be very traditional with the imposition of the notion that "if hasn't been done in the past then it should not be done." A terrible example occurred in a hill tribe in our area when a farmer fell into a fire severely burning himself. The village elders conferred to determine who had offended the spirits. They noted that one of the farmers had planted his rice in a nontraditional manner and thus he must have been guilty of causing the spirits to seek revenge. His punishment suppressed the innovative impulse that so seldom rears its head in tribal societies.

This same type of restriction of innovation and free inquiry is the subject of Ajami's books, especially *The Dream Palace of the Arabs* and *The Arab Predicament*. For the past several hundred years inventions and innovations have been common in some countries but, as he notes, in the Arab world not a single significant invention or innovation has occurred in the past 500 years. If true, this is a rather serious indictment and calls for reform. As Bernard Lewis has written, the Arab World has immediate problems that only a culture of freedom can correct.

The evil spirits that dominated the culture of the hill

CHAPTER 4

tribes where I worked for several years were always out to do harm to the villagers by acting in a capricious manner. Capriciousness was also a feature of the culture of Saudi Arabia where I also had the opportunity to work. One of my colleagues commented once that he never fully understood the real meaning of "capricious" until he had worked for a time in Saudi Arabia. One factor that contributes to the sense of capriciousness in the Middle East is the autocratic form of government. Since they have absolute power they can make whatever laws they please, whenever they please. Another factor is found in the religious system, which allows a religious cleric to have supreme power over the religious affairs. Since he speaks with the authority of God he can make whatever ruling he pleases. An example of this is seen in Iran where it has been decreed that marriage can take place for just one day, thus permitting what amounts to a thriving prostitution business.

The rigidity of traditionalism, combined with the uncertainties of capriciousness, hinder a culture seeking to be free. The transition to a society free from the constraints of tribalism seems to be no easy task, but the effort must be made to enter the modern world. The acutely increasing problems of the Arab world—as outlined so helpfully by Lewis in *The End of Modern History in the Middle East*—demand solutions that only an innovative and free thinking society can solve.

The example of Japan, which, even today remains a strictly tribal society is an interesting study in progress to modernity. Two hundred years ago that "hermit kingdom" decided that it needed to join the modern world so Western technology was imported with a passion; thus creating what has become the second largest economic power in the world while at the same time maintaining its strict form of tribalism. This tribalism though has the strength of being a unified "one tribe" country. Japan had the advantage of having a religion and culture that did not impede their march to the modern world.

America is a more interesting story in that it is a country formed of many ethnic groups but without the influence of tribalism. The primary founders of the country came from European countries where tribalism had long ceased to be the dominant cultural force. America became known as a "melting pot" where people from another country could become an "American." One of the primary influences in this process was the influence of religion in creating what

CHAPTER 4

has become known as the American Creed. This creed, with which Americans overwhelmingly agree, according to historian Samuel Huntington, includes: liberty, democracy, individualism, equality before the law, constitutionalism and private property. Though America has numerous cultural fault lines, it's adherence to these creedal principles has given the American people unity and unparalleled opportunities for innovation and freedom of inquiry.

Against this backdrop we find countries like Afghanistan, where unity has been attempted without success because of the intense tribalism existing there. In the late eighties I had the opportunity to witness the courage and bravery of some of the brightest of their young men as they trained in our school near Peshawar as medics to return to their land torn by the Soviet invasion. Those young Afghans had aspirations of creating a country unified and free, but the oppressive tribal system allowed the Taliban to gain the upper hand and descent into cultural chaos was the outcome. There were a few bright lights in that part of the world; but they were snuffed out by a tribalism dominated by radical religious ideology.

It is an interesting study to search for the factors that led the ancient Greeks out of tribalism and into a culture where free inquiry and philosophical development was, and is even today, such an inspiration. Their scientific and architectural wonders amaze those who behold the remains of their civilization. For two hours one day I wandered about the fantastic ruins of Palmyra enthralled by the sight of results of the creative minds that dwelt in those Greeks and Romans of two thousand years ago. Their struggle in the search of truth was often fraught with dangers, as Socrates found when he was forced to drink the hemlock. That was his punishment for offending the gods of his day. Indeed, the image of his sacrifice comes to mind when watching the modern day Syrian youth protestors bravely offer their lives as they strive for a society based on truth. Rather than the hemlock of Socrates, however, they face the guns of their own "god," that of Assad and his autocratic regime.

The point here is that cultures have developed, and still may develop, to a point where freedom provides the essential ingredient that allows a creative spirit to thrive. History is replete with examples where a serious price has been required for the victory gained.

CHAPTER 4

The Biblical narrative relates the steps needed to escape the inward looking obsession of tribalism. God's promise to Abraham was that "his seed would be a blessing to all peoples," was a radical departure from the inward oriented tribal culture of that era. Found in the laws of Moses are repeated injunctions to love the alien and offer the alien all the benefits of the native culture. For that time and place, such an imperative was another radical departure from the constraints of tribalism. Jesus of Nazareth was born into an intensely tribal culture and fought its regressive constraints throughout his brief lifetime. Eventually he was crucified because his society could not accept any divergence from the religious tribal system of his day.

CAPRICIOUSNESS AND THE CREATIVE SPIRIT
-CHAPTER 5-

On a village survey trip to the Karen Hill tribes we sat one evening in the light of candles discussing the problem of evil spirits. The man of the house admitted that he had never seen an evil spirit but he was deathly afraid of them. The reason for his fear was that the spirits, acting in a capricious manner, were always out to harm them.

In a corner of every village yard is a spirit house where offerings are regularly made in an attempt to appease the spirits. When an adverse event of some sort occurs, detective work must be done to determine the cause of the spirits' provocation. Anyone in the village who has recently done something contrary to custom would naturally be accused of irritating the spirit and that person would be fined in some way. Over time, the spirits developed a distinctly capricious nature, or that is the way the villagers saw the situation.

The Wa tribe of northern Burma, which I visited, had an encounter with the spirits, who seduced them into collecting human heads with the notion that such was the key to insuring a good crop of food. This belief created a great deal of trouble for them, both in the effort to collect heads and in protecting themselves from the headhunting propensities of their neighbors. Some villages came in contact with Christian missionaries and gave up their head hunting. Later, when Communism entered the area, it smothered the remaining headhunting practices. Headhunting, nevertheless, was another of the manifestations of the capriciousness of tribal animism.

Working in Saudi Arabia in the early eighties we found another culture permeated with a capricious atmosphere. Though animism was not the basis for that culture, I was reminded of the situation in the Hill Tribes of Thailand and Burma. One good example of the situation there was when a couple, both employees of our parent company, Whittaker,

CHAPTER 5

went on an outing to the Red Sea. Tragically the husband drowned, leaving a wife who was eight months pregnant. She was apprehended by the police and imprisoned because someone had to be guilty of the mishap. This was very similar to the kind of thinking found in the spirit-burdened Hill Tribes where we had worked in Thailand. Officials from our company made the trip to the town on the sea and were able to rescue the pregnant, distraught wife.

A culture where capriciousness thrives is one where rational thought is not the norm. The young man in Tunisia who set himself alight had run up against an irrational system that had led him to a dead end. While studying at the University of Texas in the mid fifties I had good friends who were from the Middle East. When discussing international situations it was evident that they did not have rational and disciplined thought processes of my Indian friends. Though the Indians had many more years of colonial rule than the Middle Easterners, they could calmly name the many things that the English had done to better their country whereas the Middle Easterners had nothing good to say about the Europeans who had briefly ruled their countries.

The capriciousness resulting from irrational thinking

has today wrought chaos on a grand scale throughout the Middle East and the Muslim world. Somalia is in the throes of a severe famine displacing millions while brutal tribal groups prevent relief to the country. Piracy on the high seas is one way of sustaining a few Somalians. Famine and anarchy griped that sad country a few years ago and the US and Western countries tried to intervene attempting to bring order and relief, but their efforts were rebuffed. The country remains a failed state while in the grip of a terrible tribal religio-political system.

Meanwhile across the sea from Somalia is Saudi Arabia with massive oil wealth, which is used to the tune of billions of dollars to build madrassas in countries like Somalia. These madrassas under the influence of the Wahhabi doctrine teach hatred toward those outside their tribe and violent jihad the likes of which is causing massive problems throughout the Middle East and other parts of the world. The massive wealth of the oil rich Middle East countries, rather than creating institutions and relief organizations with which to aid the more needy countries in the area, are spending billions creating, where land is plentiful, mile high towers.

The hopes of many for a new order evolving from the recent "Arab Spring" is already producing groans of pessimism

CHAPTER 5

as fears rise that tribalism may cause fragmentation of the cultures once unified under the heavy hands of autocracy. Yemen was a few years back divided into Communist and non-communist sections and now faces the threat of fragmenting along tribal lines and the same is the situation in Libya, and Syria.

In Egypt the dust has settled and the streets cleaned up from their protests but has anything changed for the better? While there has been a massive flight of capital from that economically starved country and the valuable tourism industry has taken a serious blow what has emerged is a combination of Military and Muslim Brotherhood to now rule the country. How will intellectual freedom, rational thinking, and liberty of conscience thrive under a system dominated by the will to primitivism?

Shiite Iran is making a play for high stakes in the area by declaring that Israel be wiped off the map. This gives them the pretense for building a nuclear bomb, which in fact would give them political dominance in that part of the world thus casting them at odds with the Sunni countries. Their support of Hezbollah in Lebanon and Hamas in the Gaza Strip further aggravates the situation in regard to Israel. These are only a few of the problems that indicate that chaos is the order of the day in the Middle East. It is tragic that the area of the world known as the cradle of civilization is now the center of chaos in the world.

The present order of chaos in the Middle East was not brought on in a day for it has been in the making for centuries. Some blame the situation on the four hundred years of the brutal hand of the Ottoman Turks who looked with disdain on the Arabs. Some of my Arab friends have blamed the brief period of Western colonialism and even the meddlesome Christian missionaries, but we must look further back to the very beginning of Islam. The tribalism that existed in the Arabian peninsula and most other parts of the world with their worship of numerous spirits or gods bred its own forms of capriciousness. The tribe's multiple gods were reduced to one god but the moral ethic of the primitive tribes was retained as a means of supporting the new religio-political system. Slavery was instituted in the new system since anyone other than the adherents of the new system was considered unworthy of living. The large number of conquered peoples who refused the new system were reduced to a servitude known as dhimmitude. For hundreds of years plundering provided the capital for the new system while slaves and the dhimmies who were a step away from slavery, provided the manpower for the new order. Chaos in the conquered lands on a scale never before seen resulted from the plundering and destroying armies. Massive numbers of slaves overwhelmed the slave markets of the capitals of Islam.

Muslims inherited lands from the Byzantines and Sassanians where there were intellectuals grounded in the Greek logical pursuit of truth as well as in the Biblical concept of a God of order and reason. For a time the ideas of the Greek philosophers with their belief in the rational order of cause and effect as well as the God of the Bible with its rational order attempted to modify the theology of Islam. Around 1000 AD the Ash'irites won the day with their belief in a god of pure will. In the Ash'rites view there is no reason, only pure will so there was no avenue for the development of logical thinking.

The enforced doctrine of the Ash'irites resulted in the "Closing of the Arab Mind" that has persisted until today. Fouad Ajami, the enlightened Arab thinker, complained that everywhere he looks in the Arab world there is the non-comprehension of cause and effect. A doctrine based on a god of pure will precludes rational inquiry into the natural order of the universe. Innovative and creative thinking is absent in such a system. People under such sway fall victims to a downhill slide into fatalism, expressed by "Inshalla" (whatever Allah wills) as we so often heard in Saudi Arabia.

Muhammad Wahhab in the mid 1700s seized the mantle of the Ash'irites and went on a campaign of "taking Islam back to the age of Muhammad". First he attacked Karbala and destroyed tombs of the Muslim prophets then conquered the Hijaz area containing the cities of Medina and Mecca slaughtering many of the inhabitants and destroying tombs of the early Muslims. Ibn al Saud teamed with him to conquer almost all of the peninsula of Arabia. Ibn al Saud's expansion was stayed by the colonial powers at that time. The radical anti-intellectual, anti-rational doctrine of the Wahhabis is the ruling doctrine of the Saudi Kingdom of today who spend billions spreading that doctrine of hate and violent jihad while at the same time keeping close to their bosom the power and technology of America and the West to stabilize their position in the Middle East.

In the mid 1950s another radical force developed in Egypt under the leadership of Sayyid Qutb. Today that force dedicated to armed jihad is the Muslim Brotherhood, which

CHAPTER 5

is a spreading influence in the Middle East. More recently the radical jihadist groups, Hamas, Hezbollah, al Qaeda and others have emerged to plague the region with their doctrines that do not tolerate free thought and innovative institutions which could provide answers to the problems of the area.

These groups promoting their own brand of tribalism and driving to extinguish free thought and liberty of conscience enforce the stratification of society, which in itself breeds chaos. Women are sequestered and given status as second-class citizens. Infidels (Jews, Christians, other religious groups and any non-Muslim) are denied an equal place in society. Slavery is still practiced openly in Sudan and tolerated in some other Middle Eastern countries. The unequal distribution of basic human rights to all in a society is a breeding ground for cultural chaos and backwardness. Dhimmitude, with its dehumanizing power, is still a part of the religio-political system dominating the Middle East. The institution of the superiority of one group over another is an infectious process smothering the spirit of freedom so necessary for innovation and creativity to thrive.

The consequences of colonialism both of the Ottoman Turks and the Western powers as well as tribalism are still touted as causes of the present sad situation of the Middle East but other countries have demonstrated that those influences can be overcome and forgotten. The fundamental problem of the Middle East is the institutionalized attack on the liberty of conscience as well as institutionalized stratification of society with basic human rights ascribed on a primitive tribal manner. As long as this persists the inheritance of the people of the Middle East will be capriciousness and chaos.

The big question that confronts us is how to get out of this institutionalized oppression that exists in the Middle East. Several hundred years ago Europe had a similar situation with the dominant churches advocating a rigid conformity to their dogma. In England in the later 1500s, a man named William Perkins began to advocate the liberty of conscience whereby a person had the God given right to believe in his heart and practice whatever he felt to be right without the imposition of a state or state church dictated dogma. The teaching of William Perkins gained traction and a hundred years later Roger Williams took up the issue in the American colonies and finally liberty of conscience was imbedded in the American constitution.

In the 1800s William Wilberforce took on the issue of

CHAPTER 5

slavery and relentlessly fought that horrible dehumanizing institution. As a member of parliament he was finally successful in banning slavery from England including English shipping. A new civility in the social order of England resulted from the efforts of Wilberforce and his compatriots.

Following the widely accepted liberty of conscience and the free inquiry of the natural order of the universe there developed in England intellectual and scientific development that was to change the world. A free wheeling association that best epitomizes the English creative spirit of that time was the "Lunar Society" composed of a loosely organized group of scientists and intellectuals who enjoyed freedom to pursue the challenge of rationally comprehending the natural order of the world they lived in. Their enterprise is best understood by describing a sampling of that group.

Joseph Priestly (1733-1804) used his inquiring mind to be one of the first to isolate and purify oxygen. He went on to isolate and describe the properties of several other gases. Because of his non-conformist religious views his library was burned and he was forced to flee to America where he lived out his life. James Watts with a keen mechanical mind took the crudely made steam engine and greatly improved the efficiency and practicality of that device making it into the driving power of the industrial revolution. William Small a physician and Benjamin Franklin both Americans were a close part of that society. Matthew Bolton and Benjamin Franklin participated in the study of electricity and sound. No subject of scientific inquiry was beyond their interest including meteorology, geology, and botany. The men of the Lunar Society met on a regular basis to freely exchange their ideas and findings. That society demonstrated what can happen when men pursue with reasoned faith the natural order of the universe. The same spirit of inquiry and creative thought inspired the Frenchman Pasteur in his many contributions to medicine including the small pox vaccine. Another Frenchman was Paschal who at the time developed the laws of hydraulics and made the first prototype of a computer.

The creations and innovations brought about by those men of the 1700s has been of great benefit and blessing to world. This was all made possible because of the struggle of men like William Perkins and William Wilberforce as they strived to throw off the yoke of tribalism with its constraining shackles on the mind. The liberty of conscience which, allowed a great era of rational discovery and development, demonstrates

CHAPTER 5

the moral imperative inherent in the creative nature of God. It was first to Abraham that God gave the directive to "be a blessing to all men." Later through the collaboration of Jethro the priest of Midian and Moses ethical laws were codified in order to direct the energies of man toward being a "blessing to all men." Those laws were intended to prevent chaos and capriciousness from infecting a society by giving all people in a society equal protection of a reasoned moral law.

Many of the laws Moses gave are today deemed irrelevant, but two are fundamental and highly relevant in today's world; laws that need to take root in the Middle East where they were first instituted. Moses dictated that all laws applied to aliens in the same manner as to his own fellow Israelites. "For remember," Moses reminded them, "you were once slaves and aliens in Egypt." Thousands of years ago as they were fleeing slavery Moses was laying down the foundational principle of what we today know as the golden rule: "Do unto others as you would want them to do to you." The law of Moses was later repeated to the Jews by Jesus in his ministry. Jesus went a step further telling his disciples to "love your enemy and pray for him." Just as tribalism had been left behind by Abraham and stripped from Moses, Jesus went about attempting to strip tribalism of its hate and revenge.

The cry for freedom in the Middle East has been loud and clear and the struggle to attain freedom has been inspiring. Yes, there has been armed and vicious struggle in some places but the struggle in Syria has been most interesting with their persistent peaceful struggle in spite of the murderous sniper fire from the autocratic government. Syria may be the moral force leading the way to a freer Middle East. Five years ago, when in Homs, Syria visiting the Central Engineering Office searching for my old college roommate, I was struck by the women, some apparently engineers, working there who were dressed as professionally as in any Western country. In contrast the women in Saudi Arabia were all sequestered in head-to-toe black burkas. For years it has been said that Christians are safer in Syria than anywhere else in the Middle East. With the Syrian's persistence in their cry for freedom it is quite possible that men after the likes of William Perkins and Roger Williams may emerge who will lead in a new cry for "liberty of conscience." Those who struggle for "liberty of conscience" to blossom in the Middle East will surely face difficulties but to bring order from the tribal chaos that sacrifice will have to be offered.

CHAPTER 5

We must look with a vision and hope that, the moral imperative inherent in the creative nature of God will be seized by those marching for freedom and will result in the stripping away of tribalism with all its institutionalized primitivism. A new order may then emerge to give freedom to innovate and create institutions that will reverse course in the Middle East replacing chaos with reasoned civilization and a modern age.

FREEDOM TO BE A CREATIVE SOCIETY
-CHAPTER 6-

Since freedom is not an end in itself we must further define its broader aspects. Some might want a society where there are no moral constraints, with no ethical rules like God has imposed in the Ten Commandments. Yet such a moral vacuum quickly devolves into an emptiness of the soul that becomes self-centered and selfish with its own enslaving capsule of futility and nihilism. True freedom does not consist in the absence of constraints, but is actually found in the moral and ethical state of the "freedom to be." Again, to understand what "to be" means we will point to the example of Abraham. Once he had been freed from tribal constraints—which have a restraining influence on one's autonomy — he was able to hear God's call "to be." That call was to be a blessing, so his freedom came in a new-found fullness of purpose and direction.

Freedom "to be," in order to have a fullness of purpose and direction in life, is contingent upon being an individual with personal autonomy, which implies liberty of conscience. The idea of personal autonomy is frightening to those within a tribal system for there is anxiety about the individual breaking out of the tribal mores, rules, and regulations, not least because doing so may result in tribal fragmentation. Though personal autonomy may be a threat to tribalism, it will strengthen one's society when used as Abraham did. He received God's call as a vocation, following God's calling to be a blessing. That relationship acted as his moral compass, thus serving as a creative force for a better society.

Creativity comes with moral obligations. The creator God, in whose image every human being is made, has commanded his imagers to "Be fruitful and increase in number; fill the earth and subdue it. Rule over the fish in the sea and the birds in the sky and over every living creature that moves on the ground" (Genesis 1:28). The moral imperative to be creative stewards over the earth gives birth to a spirit

CHAPTER 6

of invention and innovation. People and cultures generally flourish where creativity is rewarded.

Charles Murray is an award-winning political scientist and statistician who studies human accomplishment in the sciences, literature, and music. As he pointed out in *Human Accomplishment: The Pursuit of Excellence in the Arts and Sciences, 800 B.C. to 1950*, personal autonomy is the foundational element in a culture defined by innovation and inventive genius. When examining societies where human accomplishment is the most prolific, he notes that it is in countries that allow autonomy of the individual to thrive.

Alexis De Tocqueville, the nineteenth-century French political historian, found the fruit of a culture where personal autonomy flourished as he toured America in 1831. He described how the Americans had created schools, societies, and institutions throughout the country without the aid of the government. Whenever needs were identified, groups of free citizens associated to develop solutions. Those associations, created to meet the needs of society, led to rapid advancement and betterment of society in many ways.

England, Europe, and America developed systems of rewards for the inventive and innovative achievements in the fields of machinery and manufacturing processes. From the beginning of the America experience property rights were guaranteed. A national patent office protected an individual's genius of invention in machinery, science, and agriculture. Copyright protection was offered in literature and music. With these intellectual property protections, Americans went on an inventive binge confident that they would benefit from their ideas and efforts. In contrast, in a tribal system the efforts of each individual belong to the tribe. Since creative genius is poorly rewarded, traditionalism and the status quo are maintained.

The profusion of creativity that De Tocqueville described in America was, many years later, demonstrated in the relationship between Booker T. Washington, a black educator whose aim was to educate the blacks of the post Civil War poverty-stricken south, and the Jewish CEO of Sears Roebuck and Company, one of the most prosperous companies of the time. Julius Rosenwald offered Washington money for his education projects, one of which was the Tuskegee Institute. Impressed with Washington's wise use of the donated funds, Rosenwald donated more money for a school program whereby community school buildings were built for blacks.

CHAPTER 6

That program resulted in the construction of 5,000 schools in 15 states. At one time one third of all black students were schooled in a building constructed with assistance from the Rosenwald Foundation. The commission to Abraham to be a blessing to all peoples was thus passed down through a poor black Southern educator and a very wealthy Northern Jewish businessman.

Another person associated with Booker T. Washington was George Washington Carver. Born of a slave mother and unknown father he caught the attention of a white family who saw potential in the young black child. His white guardians helped him get an education, then gain admission to the University of Iowa, where he earned a masters degree in agricultural science. Rather than accept a position on the faculty, he yielded to the invitation of Washington to teach at Tuskegee Institute. He purged any resentment about slavery and segregation from his soul as he embraced a passion to help the poor ignorant blacks of the rural south. The lowly peanut was at that time mostly food for animals, but Carver saw more potential in the high protein content of the peanut and so began teaching the methods of cultivation, researching more uses of that valuable food. His invention, peanut butter, is now one of the most popular foods in the world.

Ottmar Mergenthaler was a young German with limited training as a clockmaker. He went to America to seek more opportunities than he had in his crowded homeland. As he worked in a machine shop he became interested in a better method of setting newspaper type. Within about five or six years he had completed building the linotype machine. The profound complexity of that machine, with its seven thousand parts, was a marvel of the printing industry for about 100 years. Arguably, it revolutionized printing more profoundly than any other invention, making newspapers and books freely available to anyone who wanted to read. Working under the patent laws of America he was confident that he would eventually benefit financially from the ideas he invested in that amazing machine.

Samuel Morse is another amazing success story. A portrait artist with an inventive and curious mind, he started tinkering with electricity and came up with the idea of sending signals through a wire. Before long "Morse Code" was being sent, first from city to city, then continent to continent. Thomas Edison took electricity a step further and came up with the incandescent light bulb.

CHAPTER 6

With individual freedom and personal autonomy as the norm, America rapidly became a land where inventions and innovations were popping up in every shop, garage, and backyard. Where two or three gathered together to discuss a problem, institutions were organized and machines created to solve those problems.

All the creative energy released was aided and abetted by the development of what has been described as the "American Creed." Politically, democracy developed where each person had a say in the process of government—"of the people, by the people, for the people." Underlying the whole system, however, was the idea of the "brotherhood of all men." Obviously, that commitment found detours in America as demonstrated by their treatment of Native Americans and chattel slavery, but because that commitment was there, over time, reform was possible. The brotherhood of all men had its origins in the Judeo-Christian belief that we are all equal under God. From the churches scattered throughout the land, in every hamlet, town, and city, the message was preached of a personal relationship with a just and righteous God who required an individual to love his neighbor as himself. The Christian concept of being in the presence of a living God and actually having Him live within produces a governor channeling the energy of personal autonomy towards a creative force, which has defined the Spirit of America.

Booker T. Washington and George Washington Carver could have let the psychological scars resulting from slavery evolve into resentment and revenge, but those remnants of tribal baggage were left behind as they went about "being a blessing." Going back even further in history we find the example of Joseph, sold into slavery by his brothers, who because of his personal integrity and the knowledge of the God of righteousness eventually became the savior of his brothers as well. Purged of revenge and resentment, he was able to tell his brothers that their deeds were meant for harm but God had ordained them for good.

Rewards should be available to those fulfilling their creative ideas; but in a creative society it is common for many to create for the sake of the common good without regard to personal gain. Such was the motivation of Booker T. Washington, Julius Rosenwald, and George Washington Carver. Freedom comes with the challenge to think in terms of the common good which is an extrapolation of the "blessing of Abraham." When free peoples start thinking in terms of the

CHAPTER 6

common good, tribalism will be left behind. Being created in the image of God, we in turn must create for others who are also created in His image.

The English orthopedic surgeon, Paul Brand, saw the pitiful plight of crippled and deformed leprosy patients in India as his fellow man and worked all his life to better their lot. He studied and identified the cause of their crippling deformities then developed surgical procedures to give function to useless hands. The surgical procedures he pioneered transformed the lives of tens of thousands of leprosy patients. His procedures were used on our leprosy patients in the little hospital where I first worked in Thailand.

During a medical survey of the war ravaged Cambodian people I had the chance to travel with Dr. Bob Simon, an emergency physician and founder of the International Medical Corps. First hand observation of that amazing organization was given to me in Peshawar, Pakistan as we trained Afghan medics to be doctors in their villages when they returned. The Corps has been a blessing to millions of desperate and impoverished people over the years and still is meeting needs in the most difficult situations. Dr. Bob has given thousands of hours and much of his own money for the organization because he has been influenced by a society dedicated to principle of the "common good."

From whatever culture and background we all have the potential of stripping ourselves of those impediments to creativity and thus becoming a being from which "flows rivers of living water."

CONCLUSION
-CHAPTER 7-

The tribal spirit has held sway for millennia in the Middle East. The twentieth and early twenty-first centuries saw the rise and fall of autocratic regimes in that region of the world. Sadam Hussein, Mubarak, and Gaddafi ruled through brutal oppression, but one by one they have been deposed. It has been a very long, dark winter of discontent. Today, however, the peoples of those countries are feeling the fresh winds of spring. An awakening is taking place. For how long, however, no one knows.

Just as nature abhors a vacuum, so cultures, nations, and states cannot long survive without leadership. In some countries, groups like The Muslim Brotherhood are only too happy to fill the gap. Yet this is to exchange one form of tribalism for another. If freedom is to prosper and grow throughout the Middle East, the spirit of invention must replace protectionism, the pursuit of the common good must replace sectarianism, and the freedom of personal expression must replace oppression.

Freedom requires responsibility, to be sure. The Middle Eastern experience of freedom may not look identical to the West's, but hopefully leaders in countries like Tunisia, Egypt, Libya, and Syria will look toward the best examples of their Western neighbors for inspiration. While far from perfect, the West has historically embodied virtues conducive to freedom. Notions of human dignity and human rights, innovation in science and medicine, habits of humanitarian charity and universal education, and creativity in the arts and music are gifts of the Western tradition.

As our friends in Syria and the Middle East navigate their way through very difficult waters, we challenge them to choose the path that will lead to the freedom they seek.

FOR FURTHER READING:

Fouad Ajami, *Dream Palace of the Arabs: A Generation's Odyssey*

Fouad Ajami, *The Arab Predicament: Arab Political Thought and Practice Since 1967*

Samuel Huntington, *The Clash of Civilizations and the Remaking of World Order*

Bernard Lewis, *The End of Modern History in the Middle East*

Charles Murray, *Human Accomplishment: The Pursuit of Excellence in the Arts and Sciences, 800 B.C. to 1950*

Michael Novak, *The Fire of Invention*

Raphael Patai, *The Arab Mind*

Philip Carl Salzman, *Culture and Conflict in the Middle East*